Prayers for Children

Illustrated by Constanze von Kitzing

BELLWOOD PRESS

Bellwood Press
401 Greenleaf Avenue, Wilmette, Illinois 60091-2844
Copyright © 2013 by the
National Spiritual Assembly of the
Bahá'ís of the United States

22 21 20 19   6 5 4 3

Library of Congress
Cataloging-in-Publication Data

Prayers for children / illustrated by
Constanze von Kitzing.
    pages cm
  ISBN 978-1-61851-032-7 (alk. paper)
 1. Bahai children—Prayers and devotions.
 2. Bahai Faith—Prayers and devotions. I. Von Kitzing, Constanze, illustrator.
  BP360.P725 2013
  297.9'3433083—dc23

                    2012046348

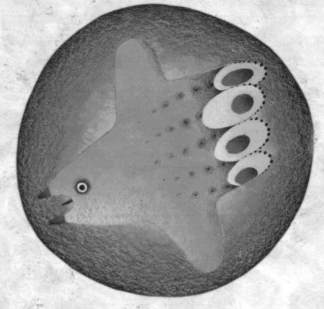

The prayers reproduced in this book can be found in *Bahá'í Prayers: A Selection of Prayers Revealed by Bahá'u'lláh, the Báb, and 'Abdu'l-Bahá* (Bahá'í Publishing Trust, 2002) and *The Summons of the Lord of Hosts* (Bahá'í Publishing, 2006).

Book design by Patrick Falso
Illustrations by Constanze von Kitzing

Preface

All over the world, every day, people say prayers. But what is prayer? Prayer can be thought of as a conversation with God. Prayer is a way for us to ask God for help when something is difficult or a way for us to thank God for all that we are grateful for. Sometimes when we are not sure what to do, a prayer can help us feel safe, connected, and inspired. In this book you will find a collection of special prayers that may help you feel closer to God. These prayers come from the Bahá'í Faith. Bahá'ís believe that there is just one God, that all of the major religions of the world come from that same God, and that all people belong to one human family.

O God, guide me, protect me,
make of me a shining lamp and a
brilliant star. Thou art the Mighty
and the Powerful.

'Abdu'l-Bahá

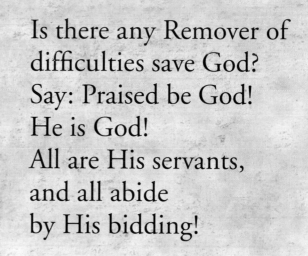

Is there any Remover of
difficulties save God?
Say: Praised be God!
He is God!
All are His servants,
and all abide
by His bidding!

The Báb

I am, O my God,
but a tiny seed which Thou hast sown
in the soil of Thy love, and caused to spring forth
by the hand of Thy bounty.

Bahá'u'lláh

I have wakened in Thy shelter, O my God,
and it becometh him that seeketh that shelter
to abide within the Sanctuary of Thy protection
and the Stronghold of Thy defense.
Illumine my inner being, O my Lord,
with the splendors of the Dayspring
of Thy Revelation, even as Thou didst illumine
my outer being with the morning light
of Thy favor.

Bahá'u'lláh

O My Lord! O my Lord!

I am a child of tender years. Nourish me from the breast of Thy mercy, train me in the bosom of Thy love, educate me in the school of Thy guidance and develop me under the shadow of Thy bounty. Deliver me from darkness, make me a brilliant light; free me from unhappiness, make me a flower of the rose garden; suffer me to become a servant of Thy threshold and confer upon me the disposition and nature of the righteous; make me a cause of bounty to the human world, and crown my head with the diadem of eternal life.

Verily, Thou art the Powerful, the Mighty, the Seer, the Hearer.

'Abdu'l-Bahá

O Thou kind Father, God! Gladden our hearts
through the fragrance of Thy love. Brighten our eyes
through the Light of Thy Guidance.
Delight our ears with the melody of Thy Word,
and shelter us all in the Stronghold of Thy Providence.

Thou art the Mighty and Powerful, Thou art the
Forgiving and Thou art the One Who overlooketh the
shortcomings of all mankind.

'Abdu'l-Bahá

Immeasurably exalted art Thou, O Lord!
Protect us from what lieth in front of us
and behind us, above our heads, on our right,
on our left, below our feet and every other side
to which we are exposed. Verily Thy protection
over all things is unfailing.

The Báb

Thy name is my healing, O my God,
and remembrance of Thee is my remedy.
Nearness to Thee is my hope, and love
for Thee is my companion. Thy mercy to me
is my healing and my succor in both this world and
the world to come. Thou, verily, art the
All-Bountiful, the All-Knowing, the All-Wise.

Bahá'u'lláh

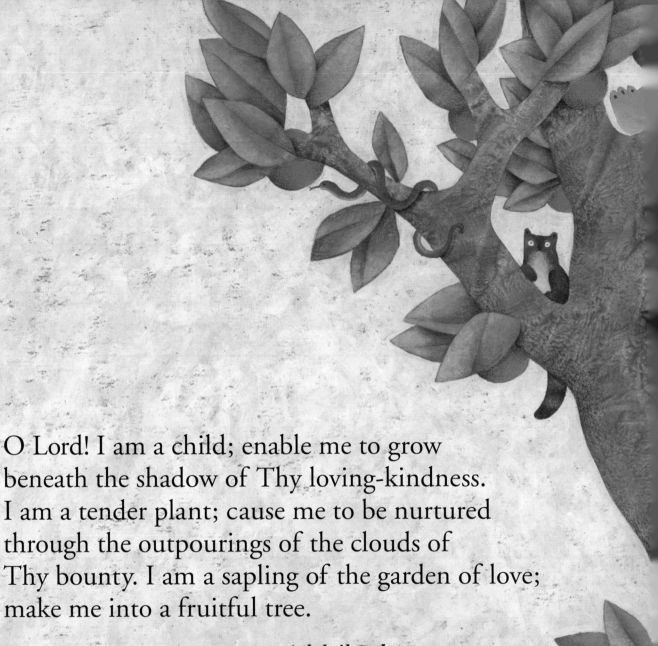

O Lord! I am a child; enable me to grow
beneath the shadow of Thy loving-kindness.
I am a tender plant; cause me to be nurtured
through the outpourings of the clouds of
Thy bounty. I am a sapling of the garden of love;
make me into a fruitful tree.

'Abdu'l-Bahá

O Lord! Grant Thine infinite bestowals, and let the light of Thy guidance shine. Illumine the eyes, gladden the hearts with abiding joy. Confer a new spirit upon all people and bestow upon them eternal life.

'Abdu'l-Bahá

O Thou the Compassionate God. Bestow upon me
a heart which, like unto a glass, may be illumined with
the light of Thy love, and confer upon me thoughts
which may change this world
into a rose garden through the
outpourings of heavenly grace.

Thou art the Compassionate, the Merciful.
Thou art the Great Beneficent God.

'Abdu'l-Bahá

O my God! I ask Thee, by Thy most glorious Name,
to aid me in that which will cause the affairs of
Thy servants to prosper, and Thy cities to flourish.
Thou, indeed, hast power over all things!

Bahá'u'lláh

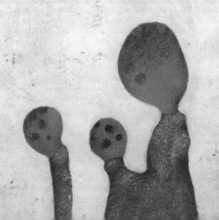

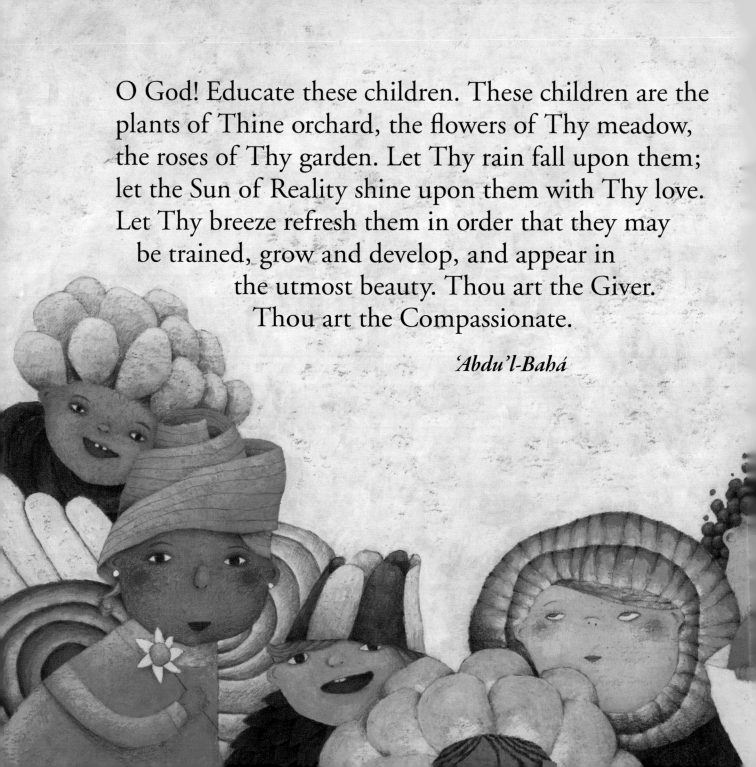

O God! Educate these children. These children are the plants of Thine orchard, the flowers of Thy meadow, the roses of Thy garden. Let Thy rain fall upon them; let the Sun of Reality shine upon them with Thy love. Let Thy breeze refresh them in order that they may be trained, grow and develop, and appear in the utmost beauty. Thou art the Giver. Thou art the Compassionate.

'Abdu'l-Bahá